The 10 Confidence Commandments

A Personal Framework for Identity, Emotional Intelligence, and Internal Alignment

Copyright Notice

Originally written as a personal confidence journal and first published under the She NetWORTH brand.

This revised edition preserves the original reflections while reflecting the author's personal and professional evolution.

Disclaimer

This book is provided for informational and educational purposes only. The content reflects the personal experiences, reflections, and perspectives of the author and is not intended as a substitute for professional, medical, legal, financial, or psychological advice.

Readers are encouraged to seek appropriate professional guidance for their individual circumstances. The author does not guarantee specific outcomes or results from the use or application of the ideas, reflections, or practices presented in this book.

All content is provided "as is," without warranties of any kind, expressed or implied. Under no circumstances shall the author be liable for any direct, indirect, incidental, consequential, or other damages arising from the use of this material.

Personal growth and confidence development are individual journeys. Outcomes may vary based on personal effort, context, and circumstances.

Foreword

This book did not begin as a framework, a methodology, or a leadership model.It began as a personal journal.

The 10 Confidence Commandments was written during a season when I was learning, sometimes painfully, how to trust myself, set boundaries, and move forward even when clarity felt out of reach. What you are holding is not a theory. It is lived experience, reflection, and lessons shaped through real life.

Over time, something unexpected happened.

As I shared these reflections with others, people saw themselves in them. They recognized the doubts, the self-talk, the exhaustion, the desire to be more grounded, more confident, more intentional. What was once personal became communal.

This book remains deeply reflective by design. It is not meant to tell you who to be or how to live. Instead, it offers ten guiding principles that invite you to pause, examine your patterns, and choose differently when needed.You may notice that some chapters feel like conversations, others like journaling prompts, and others like gentle challenges. That is intentional. Confidence is not built through information alone; it is built through awareness, honesty, and action.

You do not need to read this book in order.

You do not need to "finish" it to benefit from it.

And you certainly do not need to be an entrepreneur, leader, or expert to belong here.

You only need to be willing to reflect.

This book has evolved as I have evolved. What has not changed is its purpose;to help you build confidence from the inside out, on your terms, in your season, and at your pace.

How to Use This Book

This book is designed to be used, not rushed.
There is no correct pace, no deadline, and no expectation that you complete every exercise perfectly, or at all. Think of The 10 Confidence Commandments as a personal guide you return to as needed, not a checklist to conquer.

1. Read What Resonates

You may feel drawn to one commandment more than the others. Follow that ins tinct. Often, the principle that makes us slightly uncomfortable is the one we need most.

You can:

- Read one chapter at a time.
- Sit with a single commandment for weeks.
- Revisit the same chapter during different seasons of life.

Your experience with this book will change as you do.

2. Write Honestly (Even If It's Messy)

Each commandment includes reflection prompts and space to think more deeply about your habits, beliefs, and reactions. This is not about polished answers, it's about truthful ones.

No one else will read your responses unless you choose to share them.
Be candid. Be curious. Be kind to yourself.

3. Apply One Thing at a Time

Confidence is built through small, consistent shifts, not dramatic overhauls.
After each chapter, ask yourself:

- What stood out to me?
- What behavior or belief do I want to examine?
- What is one small action I can take this week?

Progress counts, even when it feels subtle.

4. Revisit Monthly

At the end of each month, reflect on how the commandments showed up in your life.

- Where did you grow?
- Where did you hesitate?
- Where do you want to recommit?

Confidence is not a destination; it's a practice.

5. Give Yourself Grace

Some chapters may feel affirming. Others may feel confronting. Both are part of the work. This book is not here to judge you; it is here to support your self-awareness and growth.

- You are allowed to pause.
- You are allowed to return later.
- You are allowed to evolve beyond old versions of yourself.

That, in itself, is confidence.

Closing Reminder to the Reader

The Confidence Commandments are not rules you follow once.

They are principles you revisit as life changes.

This book will meet you differently each time you open it, and that is exactly how it was meant to work.

The Confidence Commandments

The 10 Confidence Commandments

A Confidently **M.A.D.E.** individual knows they are 'Marvelous All Day Everyday.' But what does that look like in practice?

What follows are ten reflections I originally wrote for myself, tools I used to take responsibility for my life, strengthen my confidence, and grow from the inside out.

This work began as a personal journal. Over time, these reflections became principles I returned to whenever I felt overwhelmed, uncertain, or disconnected from myself. They were never meant to be a formula for success, but a foundation for self-leaders, rooted in clarity, emotional ownership, and intention.

The Confidence Commandments are not about becoming someone else. They are about coming home to yourself.

Commandment One: Take Responsibility for Yourself

Get to Know Yourself

It's easy to assume you know yourself. After all, who could possibly know you better... than you? While it's true that you probably have a wonderfully complex understanding of your desires, motivations, and strengths, it's also true that self-reflection is painful, and so is change.

So while we're uniquely equipped to know ourselves, we're also naturally inclined to protect ourselves and avoid painful experiences. This can keep us in the dark and cause us to develop "blind spots." Getting to know yourself is challenging and rewarding, resulting in greater wisdom, maturity, and confidence.

Remember to be specific as you self-reflect. Ask yourself:
What are my guiding principles?

Some examples of principles are:

- Striving for excellence
- Celebrating diversity
- A growth mindset
- Taking responsibility
- Communicating thoughtfully
- Staying relentlessly focused
- Putting distractions in their place

Write your answers down. This way, you can check in with yourself regularly to ensure your "guiding principles" are actually guiding the way!

Next, ask yourself: What is my purpose?

It sounds like it should be easy, but it's not! Do we have one purpose the whole way through? Can your goal change? These are relevant questions and worth exploring at length. Don't feel bad if nothing immediately comes to mind. The whole point of self-reflection is getting to the bottom of things.

You might decide that your purpose is incredibly specific, like opening an empanada bakery to keep your family's secret recipe alive. Or, your answer might be more broad, like helping revitalize your community through your art. When it comes to your purpose, there is no wrong answer.

Figure Out What You Want

Figuring out what you want ties into knowing your principles and purpose. Translating your "why" into your "what" is the natural progression of self-reflection. Maybe you want to do work that's satisfying and rewarding. Or perhaps you want to use your natural gifts to improve the world around you.

The more you explore your "why" and "what," the more specific your goals will become. Questions lead to answers which lead to new questions. Eventually, you will discover specific ways to put your ideas and talents to work in your everyday life.

Ask yourself: What's worth doing even if I fail? This is an excellent place to start as you hone in on what you want.

Accept Your Reality

Dreams and reality are not at odds. If you've seen someone constantly dreaming but never doing, it's not because realizing your aspirations is impossible. It's because visions don't come to life through warm feelings. They come to life through work, perseverance, and diligence.

As distressing as it might sound, accepting your reality starts with admitting your flaws. This is not the same as shaming yourself or beating yourself up. Humble people see the full picture: all their weaknesses and failures, brilliance and potential. And because they're honest about where they need to grow, they are constantly evolving. The question is never whether we have flaws.

The question is how our weak points are standing in the way, causing harm, or keeping us stuck, and what we're going to do about it.

Stay True to Yourself

It's not all flaws and weaknesses! Accepting your reality also means embracing your talents, unique traits, winning qualities, and potential. When you can sit with the complete picture of who you are without condemnation, you can truly start to love yourself.

It can be helpful to speak to yourself as you might a young child. You don't want to enable bad behavior, but you also don't want to humiliate or terrify. Loving yourself means leaving space for mistakes, setbacks, and even failures. Don't just look at how far you are from your goal. Look at how far you've come along the way.

Know When to Take Care of Yourself

The conversation around self-care can be a confusing one. Isn't it selfish to place yourself above everyone else? If everyone did that, wouldn't the whole world fall apart? Sometimes, the narratives we see around self-care seem shallow. Certainly, it's more than a bubble bath and a trip to the mall?

True self-care is about supporting yourself in meaningful ways. Self-care isn't selfish because it is only when we are rested, nourished, supported, and empowered that we can effectively show up to love and help others.When you realize that self-care doesn't end with the self, you catch a glimpse of how critical it really is. And hey – sometimes it DOES mean a bubble bath and a trip to the mall. It's just that it's also so much more.

EXERCISE: Set Your Guiding Principles
TIME IT TAKES: 30 minutes to 1 hour, plus regular review

Embrace the essence of personal responsibility by taking ownership of your values, as it stands as one of the most pivotal elements. Let's dive deeper into your Guiding Principles, prepare a fresh cup of coffee and eagerly turn the page to embark on the invigorating exercise awaiting you on the next page...

1. What is a priority (or priorities) that speaks to my soul? (For example: follow my calling, never stop learning, live with confidence, give back, etc.)
2. What is it about this priority that resonates with me?
3. What words come to mind when I meditate on this priority?
4. Why is this priority special or important?
5. How does honoring this priority benefit others?
6. What are some specific times I lived in accordance with this priority and how did they make me feel?

These priorities are your guiding principles. They rest at the foundation of who you are and why do you what you do. It's okay to start with one. In fact, too many principles can get confusing.

Now that you know your guiding principle(s), check in with yourself nightly or weekly to see how aligned you feel with those priorities. If you aren't living out of the guiding principle you WANT, consider what's actually motivating you. Is it fear? Anxiety? People-pleasing?

Regularly review your guiding principles and be sure to add new ones as they become clear.

Set Your Guiding Principles

What is a priority that speaks to my soul?

What about this priority resonates with me?

What words come to mind when I think about this priority?

What makes this priority special or important?

How does this priority benefit others?

Specific moments I lived in alignment with this priority:

Additional Notes

Commandment Two: The Fine Art of Saying No

Isn't It Mean to Say No?

No! But it's easy to oversimplify the matter. For example, you might avoid saying no because you hate disappointing people. After all, isn't it cruel to disappoint people? Not necessarily.

There's a lot to unpack regarding expectations and requests, but the short answer is: It depends.

Let's look at a few scenarios:

Your neighbor asks you to house-and-cat-sit 48 hours before they go out of town for two weeks. Their original sitter fell through, and they can't find anyone else last minute. But you work full-time away from home, have an hour-long commute, and are allergic to cats.You don't work Sundays, but your boss sends you "emergency tasks" on Sundays. They knew about your boundary up-front, but they're hoping it's flexible "as needed."

A family member asks you to do something you feel is unethical. Everyone else in your family thinks it's harmless and makes a fuss, calling you difficult.

In all of the scenarios above, and a million more, it's more than okay to say no–it's healthy. Unfortunately, you don't have to be a "people-pleaser" to place a high value on cooperation and peace. As such, "yes" might be your go-to response.

But you can say "no" for any reason you like. Whether you're tired, stressed, they're crossing a boundary, you have too much on your plate, or you just don't feel like it, knowing your limits is essential.

For example, you might say "no" like this:

Unfortunately, I'm not able to take this on right nowI appreciate your consideration, but my schedule won't permit it at this time.

What you're doing sounds exciting, but now is not the right time for me.

I don't have the bandwidth for that request, but I know someone who might
I'm sorry; I can't give that request the time it deserves right now.

Remember: No matter how much you trust someone, they have their own biases and motivations. They see things through the lens of THEIR wants and needs. And they won't know or understand YOURS unless you tell them.

Why Are You Saying Yes?

One of the most helpful exercises as you get comfortable saying "no" is to analyze the reason behind your "yes."

Does any of this sound familiar?

- If I say no, this person might fire me/break up with me/stop being my friend.
- If I say no, this person might get mad at me.
- If I say no, this person might think I'm selfish.
- If I say no, this person might be disappointed in me.

Do you see a theme? Most of these thoughts aren't reasons to say "yes"–they're fears around saying "no." While fear is natural and valid, being afraid of the consequences is generally a lousy reason to say "yes" to something.

Try asking, "If I wasn't afraid of angering or upsetting this person, would I still say yes?" It can also be helpful to remember that people frequently make their requests sound urgent, even when they're not. That's because they know how many voices are vying for your attention, and urgency is one of the best ways for them to stand out.

Benefits of Saying No

It's common for people to think that saying "no" will be the beginning of the end. But saying "yes" out of fear creates burnout and resentment, lowering your quality of life.

You might have heard it said, "Say no to everything so you can say yes to the one thing." The idea is that we neglect critical aspects of our life when we make "yes" our default answer for every request.

Benefits of saying "no" include:

- It can help you distance yourself from users and abusers.
- You'll make much better use of your time.
- You're practicing a critical form of self-care.
- It's a sign of respect–for yourself AND the other person.
- You're setting a positive example for others

One fascinating aspect of learning to say "no" is discovering that most requests aren't bad. It's far more likely someone will ask you to dinner than for help robbing a bank. So saying "no" isn't personal, nor does it reflect negatively on the asker.

The secret? You have to say "no" to a lot of good things so you can show up fully and authentically for the two or three things that matter the most–the very BEST things. People of integrity will understand and respect this concept.

Commandment Two: The Fine Art of Saying No

EXERCISE: Name Your YES
TIME IT TAKES: 15 - 30 minutes, plus regular review

One of the best ways to fine-tune the practice of saying no is to name your YES. To me, this means honing in on one, two, or three things that take precedence over everything else. For example, your YES could be your family, your business, and your health. Or, your YES could be your art and your spiritual practice.

Your YES priorities are non-negotiable and tower high above everything else. Or at least, they should. Often, our actions fall out of alignment with our values, and we find ourselves in distress. Usually, this happens because we can't say NO to all the things that divide us, distract us, and take away from our YES.

Grab a fresh journal or create a document that you can dedicate to decisions. For each decision, leave space for the following considerations:

1) Do I feel like I have to say yes? If so, why?
2) What feeling is motivating me in this decision?
3) If I agree to do this, is it at the expense of my YES?
4) Does my ego have any role in this decision? For example, would saying yes help me feel needed or important?
5) What kind of example am I setting if I say yes?
6) How does saying yes to this particular ask nurture my bigger YES?
7) Am I the only one who can say yes?
8) Do I know someone else who is a better fit for this ask?
9) Does the thought of saying yes make me feel anxious, tense, or sick to my stomach?
10) What would happen if I said no?

Once you've explored your feelings around each decision, meditate on your YES for one to two minutes. Whether it's a favor, a job, an opportunity, or an invitation, does this ask feel like it aligns with and supports your YES? Or does it feel like it competes, detracts, and diminishes from your top priorities?

Here, you will almost always find your answer.

An invigorating exercise is awaiting you on the next page.

Name Your 'YES'

Do I feel like I have to say yes? If so, why?

What feeling is motivating this decision?

Would agreeing interfere with my yes?

What kind of example would my "yes" send?

How does this yes nurture my bigger YES?

Am I the only one who can say yes/do I know a better fit?

Does the thought of saying yes make me feel anxious, tense, or sick?

What would happen if I said no?

Final Thoughts:

Commandment Three: Experiment with Life

Explore Diverse Opportunities for Growth

Experimenting is often misunderstood as something we outgrow—but growth doesn't follow a deadline. There seems to be an unspoken rule that experimenting is for people who haven't "figured it out yet." We can even assign negative connotations to experimentation, wondering whether people who try new things are "lost" or "confused."

But there is no expiration date for experimentation! The idea that we should know who we are and what we want by our early 20s is misguided. Many of us are placed in specific boxes by our families, communities, or SELVES. As such, people can be well into their 30s or 40s (or older!) before they come into their own.

Consider the following scenarios:

1. A widower becomes a professional landscape photographer in her mid-sixties. She pays off her mortgage and supports herself through her art.
2. A man enters the real estate field in his late forties after losing his job in retail management. Within five years, he is one of the top-selling residential realtors in the United States.
3. A woman in her seventies begins acting in her local theater—something that was always discouraged by her family. She has immense talent and is praised

It's natural to think you should have things figured out by a certain age or season. At every turn, society reinforces this idea. And it's comforting to stay on well-worn, familiar paths where we feel capable and safe. **risk, failure, and experimentation.**

But growth comes out of

When you think of those three words, what emotions come to mind?

Fixed VS Growth Mindset

Whether or not you experiment could come down to your mindset. While it's impos sible to reduce all of humanity into two categories, there are two mindsets that can help us understand how we view risk, failure, and experimentation.

A fixed mindset believes:

- I'm either good at something, or I'm not!
- Intelligence, talents, and abilities do not change over time!
- Making mistakes is humiliating!
- The best way to avoid failure is to stop trying new things!
- If I don't master something immediately, it means I'm not cut out!
- Failure is a sign that I should give up!

By contrast, a growth mindset believes:

- Mistakes are the only way anyone learns!
- To improve, I have to keep pushing myself and trying new things!
- I will fail along the way, but that's all part of growing!
- When I fail, I use the lessons I've learned to try again!
- The only true failure is giving up out of fear!
- I celebrate small achievements because they lead to big successes!

If you find trying new things overly frightening or distressing, you might be operating with a fixed mindset. The good news is you can shift your perspective toward growth.

Leave Your Comfort Zone

One of the best ways to leave your comfort zone is to adopt a growth mindset. Like any new habit, it takes time, patience, and dedication–but it opens up a whole new world of possibilities.

Here are three ways to shift your mindset and step out of your comfort zone:

1. **Be intentional with your language.** The stories we tell ourselves are powerful, so you can start by shifting how you talk about failure, experimentation, and risk. This doesn't mean putting a positive spin on everything, a la "toxic positivity." It means rejecting old patterns of negativity and self-sabotage in favor of a healthier perspective.

2. **Seek Feedback.** Genuine growth thrives on supportive, wise feedback. Specifically, get feedback from people who have accomplished what you want to do. See feedback as someone believing in you enough to invest in you, but remember–they're only one source among many.

3. **Ask for help.** Maybe you've heard the saying, "If you want to get somewhere fast, go alone. If you want to go further, go together." It can be scary to seek outside guidance, but it's also essential. A growth mindset values mentorship, coaching, and accountability groups because they rapidly accelerate growth.

Changing how you talk about failure, accepting feedback, and prioritizing outside learning are effective ways to adopt a growth mindset.

There will be discomfort at first as you lean into unknown territory, but your new perspective and support system will create significant momentum! As it does, you'll realize you're more resilient, talented, and powerful than you ever imagined.

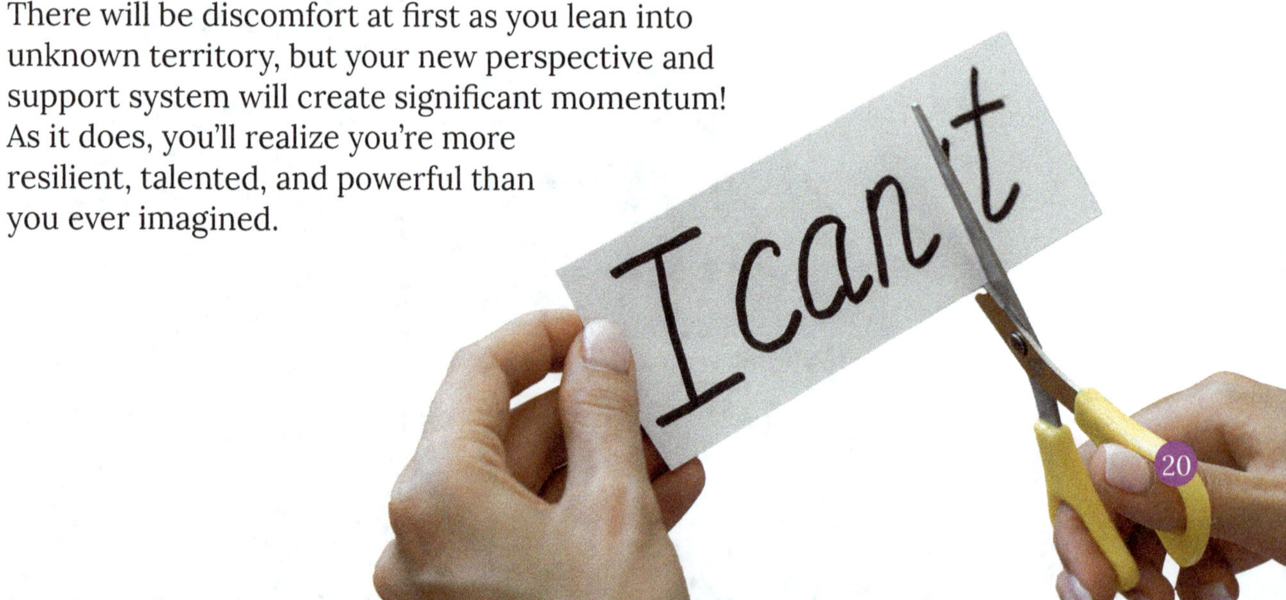

Commandment Three: Experiment with Life

Exercise: Make a Date With Risk
TIME IT TAKES: A few minutes to a few hours, at least once a month.

Don't worry; this isn't as scary as it sounds. Making a date with Risk isn't about skydiving or eating squid–unless you want it to be!

Experimentation is all about getting out of your comfort zone so you can expand your understanding of yourself, others, and the world around you. There's a saying: Run toward what scares you. It simply means that living small makes us smaller, and stepping out in faith forces us to evolve.

At least once a month, make a date with Risk and KEEP IT. Start small, so you aren't overwhelmed. It's up to you to prioritize which kinds of risks are going to be most beneficial to your personal growth. Usually, what scares us the most is a great indicator of where we need to go.

Each time you take a risk, ask the following questions:

1) What is the risk? (This could be as big as moving to a new town or as practical as speaking up in a meeting.)
2) How does the risk align with my values?
3) If I don't take this risk, will I regret it?
4) What's the worst that could happen?
5) What might stop me from taking this risk?
6) Will this change my life for the better?

Follow up later and add updates on where your risk has led you. Explore these questions each time you take a chance to see what's motivating you, what's holding you back, and how taking risks can transform your life in surprising ways. Be sure to use the exercise on the next page as your guide.

Make A Date With Risk

What is the risk?	How does the risk align with my values?
If I don't take the risk, will I regret it?	What's the worst that could happen?
What might stop me from taking this risk?	Will this change my life for the better?

Additional Notes

Commandment Four: Develop Clear Goals + An Action Plan

Defining Your Goals

Clarity becomes powerful when it's rooted in intention, not pressure. While it's easy to assume you HAVE goals, if you try to define them, you might discover they're not as fleshed-out as you thought.

That's why one of the most critical aspects of goal-setting is to be specific. When you get up close and personal with your goals, and map steps to accomplish them, you take your aspirations from "dream" territory into reality.

Setting goals:

- Gives you motivation for the short-term
- Offers a vision for your future
- Is linked to successful outcomes
- Gives your life essential direction
- Helps you establish and rank priorities
- Boosts self-esteem, self-confidence, and self-reliance

Write It Down

The best way to identify and clarify your goals is to write them down. Go ahead, get yourself a Goal Journal! But before you sit down to write, take some time to reflect. Think about what you want to achieve and why. And don't be surprised if your goals surprise you!

For example, you might think your primary goal is to pay off your debt. But upon reflection, you could realize your primary goal is to buy a house, and paying down debt is one of several milestones along the way.

Try creating goal categories like:

- Family or home-life
- Professional or career
- Fitness and nutrition
- Spiritual
- Creative or artistic
- Personal growth

By defining and owning your goals, you're setting yourself up for success. You can also celebrate smaller milestones along the way to accomplishing specific goals.

Once you've identified your goals in writing, list the benefits, set some time targets, and detail how you plan to achieve each goal. Keep your Goal Journal close by so you can make updates and additions regularly. The details and specifics will morph and meander a little along the way, so adjust accordingly and keep going!

Stick With It

If achieving goals was a walk in the park, everyone would do it! Goal setting and meeting require consistency, accountability, and dedication. The good news is the more you practice these qualities, the more they will become second nature.

As you progress toward your goals and even accomplish them, you'll find your motivation and enthusiasm reaching new heights. This momentum will fuel your next dream. And the next, and the next...

It's best to start with small, achievable goals. This way, you can enjoy the excitement and satisfaction of seeing them through. Later, you can build on those bite-sized goals because your "diligence and dedication muscles" will be stronger than ever.

Act "As If"

Acting "as if" is a great way to exercise your imagination and realize your goals. After all, it's no secret that if we want to create new lives we have to embrace new thinking.

Acting "as if" works like this:

1 Act as if the mindset you desire is already in-place. For example, if you were incredibly confident or resilient, what would you be thinking and doing right now? This exercise in mental exploration will cause your mindset to evolve, eventually making you more confident, resilient, etc.

2 Act is if you were a specific person (mentor, family member, historical figure, public figure) who has achieved what you want to achieve. Try to imagine what that person would say or do in a similar situation. Remember, it's not about imitation. It's about honing in on specific qualities and outcomes and keeping them front-and-center in your mind.

Acting "as if" will take you out of your comfort zone at first. That's a good thing! As you learn to act out of your new mindset, you will develop and strengthen the very characteristics you admire. Eventually, you won't be acting "as if." You will be the YOU you always imagined.

Commandment Four: Develop Clear Goals + An Action Plan

EXERCISE: Create an Action Plan Blueprint
TIME IT TAKES: 30 minutes to 1 hour for each action plan

Knowing your goals is great. But unless you have an action plan, you're unlikely to see the progress you want. Creating an Action Plan Blueprint is an excellent way to map your intentions and better understand how you can make them a reality

1) **Define your goal.** Write it down. Get specific. Brainstorm away: How will you get from here to there? Break it down step-by-step. Now you can.

2) **List the smaller** tasks on the way to accomplishing your main goal. Give each task a "doable" due date. Take time to consider how long each task will realistically take.

3) **Assign tasks.** Tasks can be assigned to you, someone else, or the responsibility might be shared. Make sure everyone involved knows their assignments and due dates. Regularly check in on task status and make alterations as needed. If a due date passes, don't let anxiety trick you into abandoning the blueprint altogether. Sit down with your action plan, reassess your strategy, assign new due dates, and keep going.

4) **Celebrate milestones.** Keep the enthusiasm and momentum going by recognizing and celebrating completed tasks on the way to your larger goal. Acknowledging your progress-even if it's just to yourself-will help you stay positive.

5) **Assess.** You've reached your goal. Fantastic! Write down everything you learned along the way. What lessons did you learn about planning versus execution? What would you have done differently? If you worked with others, collect feedback and jot it all down.

Now you're ready for the next goal, the next action plan, and the next success! Flip to the next page and begin creating your BLUEPRINT!

Action Plan Blueprint

Define your goal:

List smaller tasks:

Assign tasks:

Celebrate milestones:

How I can act "as if":

Assess:

Additional Notes

Commandment Five: Live Your Purpose

Know Your Why

Only some people value and believe in purpose. If you've read this far, I'm inclined to think you're a believer! But among people who appreciate and prioritize purpose, you can find individuals who feel certain and individuals who feel lost at sea.

Knowing your WHY is an excellent way to gain clarity, whether you know your purpose or feel like you've been searching for it like buried treasure. After all, even people who seized their purpose long ago can feel disoriented at times.

Consider the following:

- What did you most enjoy as a child?
- What activities cause you to enter a flow state–losing time, feeling energized, experiencing rare clarity, and enjoying immense satisfaction?
- What makes you angry?
- Where do your skills, passions, and innate talents point?
- Who do you admire, and why?
- Where do your abilities intersect with a need you see in the world?
- What topics, activities, or themes make you feel on fire?

Pablo Picasso said, "The meaning of life is to find your gift. The purpose of life is to give it away." Journaling your answers to the above questions is an excellent exercise for knowing, clarifying, or remembering your purpose.

Be a Lifelong Learner

A big part of living your purpose is learning. Most people with a strong sense of pur pose are in pursuit of excellence–they don't just want to do something; they want to master it. To achieve this level of skill, you must stay teachable.

In addition to learning everything you can about your vocation, craft, or mission, it's also helpful to remain flexible on the details.

Being a lifelong learner means staying open to the possibility that your dream:

- Might take longer than you expected.
- Might be bigger than you imagined.
- Might require more sacrifice than you thought.
- Might involve people you never considered.

As a lifelong learner, you're not just improving your skills and competency. You're learning to be adaptable, versatile, and resilient enough to keep up with the exhilarating pace of your dreams.

Empower Others

Purpose is always about people. If it isn't about people, it's not your purpose. The composer who works in solitude? The researcher who spends more time with Petrie dishes than human beings? At the end of the day, they're doing it for people.

The composer is in service of the listener. The researcher is in service of scientific advancements that create a better quality of life–for people. Again, ask yourself where your passion and skills align with a great need you see in the world.

Whether you're going to shine a light by cooking comfort food or creating code, someone else always benefits when you're operating out of your purpose.

Volunteer

Volunteering is a beautiful way to honor and hone your purpose. Why? Because purpose is always about serving others. People who step fully into their purpose are all about advancing, healing, uplifting, supporting, and helping others.

When we volunteer our time, attention, and resources, we develop an internal posture of service and humility. These attitudes can help us stay faithful to our calling and keep others at the center of all we do.

Be Grateful

Being grateful every step of the way is essential. If you wait for specific achievements to express gratitude, you'll spend a lot of time feeling dissatisfied.

Significant milestones happen occasionally, but your life's work is before you every day. If you can find joy and gratitude in the everyday, you'll develop an attitude that allows you to enjoy not just the destination but the journey.

You can hone the fine art of gratitude by:

1 **Thanking others.** Try embracing the old-fashioned tradition of handwritten notes! The extra time and thoughtfulness go a long way. Plus, writing things by hand has been shown to clarify emotions and clear your mind.

2 **Keeping a journal.** Gratitude has a way of multiplying. You might sit down thin king you're going to write down three or four things you're grateful for, and the next thing you know, you've listed twenty-three. The result? You feel even more thankful than when you sat down to write!

3 **Be still and reflect.** It's easy to feel inundated by requests, demands, and expectations, leading to burnout and stress. Carving out time to listen and reflect can do wonders for our perspective. When the noise subsides, we often our souls' quiet joy and rejoicing.

A **gratitude challenge** is an exciting way to invite thankful ness into your life. Dedicate a fresh notebook to writing down things that make you happy for three weeks. Try to write three a day, but don't stop there if the ideas keep coming!

After three weeks, you might decide this is a habit worth keeping. From the smell of rain to harmonica solos to that square of dark cho colate you found in your desk drawer, life's little (and big!) gifts really are everywhere.

EXERCISE: 21-DAY GRATITUDE CHALLENGE
TIME IT TAKES: A few minutes a day

A three-week gratitude challenge can transform your outlook and your attitude! It can also help you live your purpose by constantly drawing your attention to things that move, inspire, and excite you.

A gratitude challenge is easy–it's basically a promise to jot down several things you're grateful for each day. I recommend keeping it simple:

1) Write down three things/people/experiences you are grateful for.

It doesn't have to be something that happened that day or the day prior; it can be anything that comes to mind.

If you'd like to dive deeper into the challenge, incorporate the following prompts into your daily practice.

2) Write someone a thank-you note.
3) Leave a five-star review online for a business or service.
4) Send someone a text telling them why you're grateful to have them in your life Or even better, give them a call!
5) Leave a special treat for the mailman.
6) If someone in your neighborhood has a garden/lawn/rose bushes that add beauty to the block, let them know you appreciate it!
7) Unfollow social media accounts that consistently make you feel bad about yourself or your life.

You get the idea! Write down things that make you grateful, then try to turn your attitude of gratitude into actions someone else can appreciate. At the end of the 21 days, use the journal on the next page to document the challenge and its results. If you found value in the practice, there's no reason it can't become a staple in your daily routine.

21-Day Gratitude Challenge

Day	What I'm grateful for today:
Day One	
Day Two	
Day Three	
Day Four	
Day Five	
Day Six	
Day Seven	
Day Eight	
Day Nine	
Day Ten	
Day Eleven	
Day Twelve	
Day Thirteen	
Day Fourteen	
Day Fiveteen	
Day Sixteen	
Day Seventeen	
Day Eighteen	
Day Nineteen	
Day Twenty	
Day Twenty One	

Commandment Six: Take Nothing (Or Very Little) Personally

What Happens When We Take Things Personally?

We've all been there: Someone says or does something, and we're on the defense in a heartbeat. Whether it was a misunderstanding, a flawed assumption, or an act of slander, communication breaks down, and all heck breaks loose!

When we take something personally, we usually feel our character, competence, abi lities, or choices are under attack. Whether that's the case or not, it's essential to re member that we have no control over what others say or feel.

So... What CAN we control, and how can we stop taking (all of the) things personally? Let's look at three ways to take our power back.

Rethink Your Thinking

Metacognition is the ability to think about our thoughts. It's a fascinating ability and essential to our personal growth. Even though it's easy to feel victimized by our thoughts, we have the capacity to capture them, examine them, and hold them accountable.

If you frequently take things personally, consider whether you might be struggling with your self-image. For example, you might be extremely sensitive to feedback on your work because you feel unqualified or suffer from imposter syndrome. Deep down, you may feel like a failure or a loser.

When we take things personally, it could be because we're letting others define who we are. But if you decide definitively who you are, what others say won't hold as much weight.

Try reinforcing and affirming positive things you know to be true about yourself.

You might include things like:

1. I am imperfect, but I try to learn from my mistakes.
2. When I am in the wrong, I seek to make amends.
3. I have made strong progress over the past few years.
4. My past mistakes do not define me.
5. Every year, my work gets better.
6. I am making solid progress toward my goals.
7. I prioritize being of service to others.

Don't Assume the Worst

Everyone knows the old saying about what happens when you assume, so I won't repeat it here! But there's a reason the act of assumption earned such an enduring (and memorable) phrase. We do ourselves (and others) a great disservice when we assume.

Misunderstandings happen all the time. Add text and email to the equation, and you've got a misunderstanding minefield. Communication can be a fine art, but it can also be a reckless mess. Tone, intention, and message are all easy to get wrong face-to-face, let alone in written exchanges.

When you hear or read something you're tempted to take personally, take a deep breath instead. Give it some space. We've all had experiences where we read or heard something one way, only to discover we missed the point entirely. Which begs the question: Is it their tone, or is it my lens?

I want to suggest something radical. Rather than assuming the worst, try imagining the best. It's not naive or ridiculous to expect the best from people. On the contrary, it can help us–and them–step into a place of greater peace and power.

Which brings us to...

Regardless of how you usually receive criticism, you probably recognize that there are two kinds: constructive and destructive. Consider the source, and you'll have a pretty good idea of which you've just experienced.

Constructive criticism is for your benefit. It doesn't involve insults, exaggerations, or sensationalism. It doesn't have a malicious or arrogant tone. A good example would be a teacher, mentor, or boss offering tips on improving your essay writing or public speaking skills.

Destructive criticism is not for your benefit. Instead, it gives the other person some kind of thrill. Maybe they want to argue, get a reaction, or prove you " aren't as put-together" as you seem. Ask yourself whether envy might be at the root, and proceed accordingly.

Your power lies, as you might have guessed, in your reaction. Constructive criticism is a gift offered for your growth and evolution. It's also an honor because it means someone is investing and believing in you. Destructive criticism is a distraction, so don't take the bait. The best reaction is no reaction.

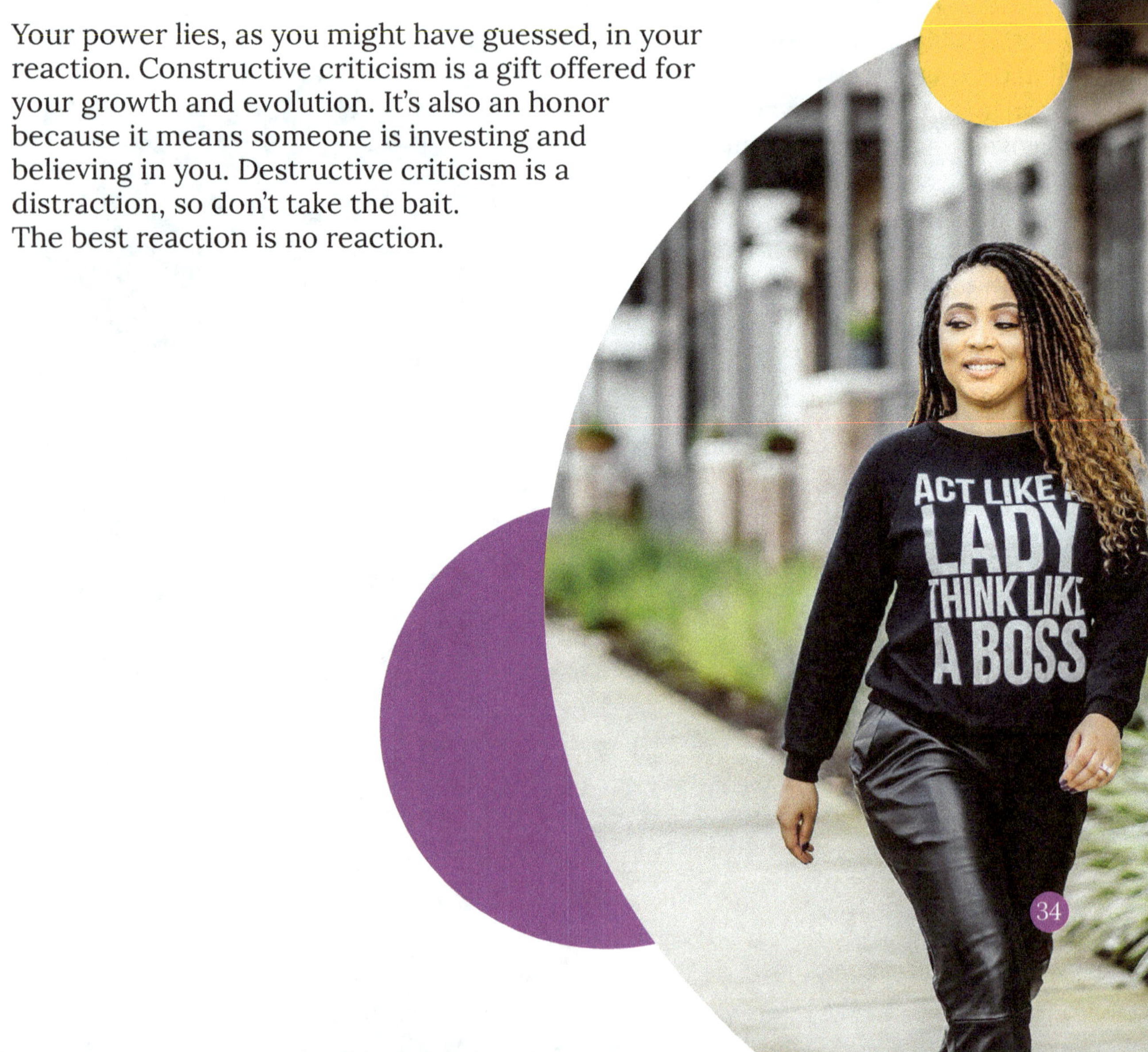

Commandment Six: Take Nothing (Or Very Little) Personally

EXERCISE: Learn Your Triggers
TIME IT TAKES: A few minutes a day

If you find yourself taking things personally quite a bit, there's a good chance you have some unresolved emotions, traumas, or feelings. A trigger, or activator, is something that disrupts these unresolved matters, almost like poking a hornet's nest.

Getting to the root of your triggers can help you identify what's happening and put it in perspective. It might not be what someone just said about your cooking or your hair; it might be "that thing" from your past sneaking up on you once again.

Work to identify your triggers by using the journal on the next page to answer the following questions:

1) What am I feeling? (Be specific. Instead of "mad" or "hurt," try " inadequate," "unworthy," "envious," or "insecure."
2) What emotions or memories arose in the minutes or hours after the "offensive" experience?
3) In light of my previous answers, is it possible I took this comment/action the wrong way?
4) Am I assuming the worst about this person/situation when there are other possible intentions or meanings?
5) Was this actually directed at me, or was the other person upset about some thing/someone else?
6) What emotions keep coming up for me each time I take something personally, and what memories keep surfacing?

Sit with your emotions for at least ten minutes and on the next page write down anything else that comes to mind. As you work through your feelings and thought processes after an offense (preferably later that day), you'll begin to see nuance and complexity.

You'll also start to feel more capable and empowered because you aren't a victim things keep happening to; you're a student learning about your internal processes and working to improve your external reactions.

Learn Your Triggers

What am I feeling?

What emotions surfaced after the experience?

Is it possible I took this "the wrong way"?

Is it possible I'm assuming the worst about this situation/person?

Was this really directed at me?

When I take something personally, what emotions keep coming up?

Additional Notes

Commandment Seven: Take Responsibility for Your Emotions

What Does it Mean to Own Your Feelings?

Owning your feelings involves acknowledging them, thinking about them, and processing them. We all FEEL our feelings, but we don't all honor and own them.

Owning your feelings can:

- Decrease aggression.
- Improve how we handle stress.
- Make us less likely to self-injure.
- Help us establish positive mental health.
- Improve our ability to handle challenging situations.

When you own your emotions, you aren't allowing them to blindside and rule you. Instead, you're thoughtfully considering how you feel. By taking a step back, you can examine your emotions, hold them accountable, and honor them.

How Do We Own Our Emotions?

Like most things, you can become better at owning your emotions with practice. When you do, you'll probably be surprised at how insightful and empowered you feel.

You can own your emotions by:

- **Letting the emotions flow.** Stifling feelings is no way to own them. When negative feelings arise, our first impulse can be to stuff them. But all emotions are valid. Instead of shaming them, sit with them and listen to what they say.

- **Expanding your emotional vocabulary.** In a survey, many people found it hard to identify more than three emotions: happiness, sadness, and anger. But the human experience is much more complex. We experience shame, overwhelm, rage, despair, delight, joy, envy, jealousy, pride, rapture, inspiration, and love. Try digging deep to say what you're genuinely feeling.

- **Talking about it.** Whether with a sibling, therapist, or friend, talk it out. Having at least one trusted confidant is essential, so you feel safe expressing your emotions. A strong support system can help you work through difficult emotions, care for your mental health, and better manage stress.

Listen

We're usually pretty good at listening to our pleasant feelings. They make us feel good, balanced, and healthy. But we also tend to label a whole host of emotions as "bad." Try rejecting the idea that any feelings are wrong and listening instead.

Here are some feelings you might label "bad":

- Envy
- Frustration
- Anger
- Agitation
- Pride
- Impatience

If you're experiencing an emotion that doesn't align with your values, know that this is totally natural. Rather than shaming yourself and stuffing the feeling, try looking at it with curiosity.

Ask what might be at the root of this emotion. Brainstorm with ideas for healthier expressions. Most importantly, know that feelings are never all good or all bad on their own. It's what we do with them that counts.

For example, if you're angry, take some time. Try to process your emotions before responding or reacting. Maybe your anger is justified, but you don't want to yell or attack because those behaviors don't align with your values. Acknowledge the anger, hear it out, and decide how to respond with since rity and grace.

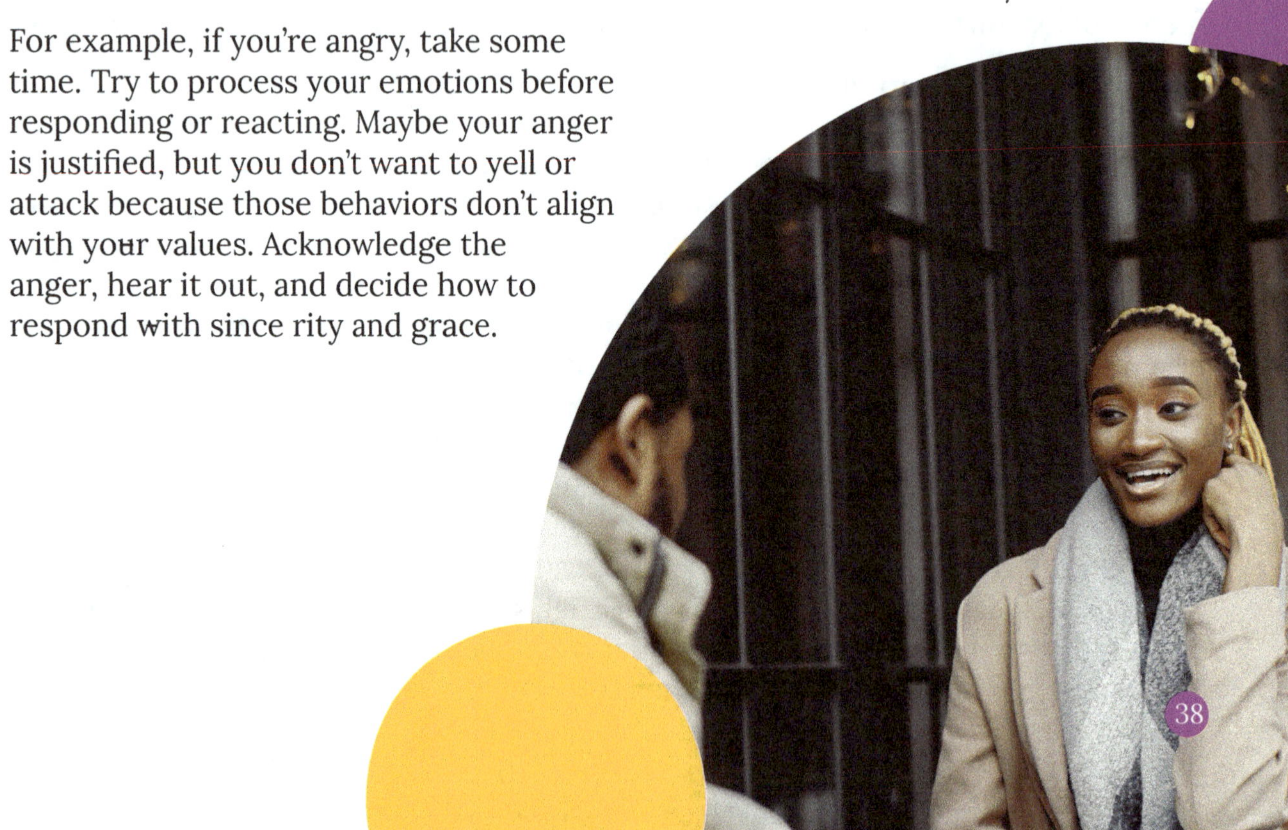

Be Open to Love

Most people think they're open to love. The shocking truth? Many of us are not.

You can know you're struggling to stay open to love when:

- You don't practice or prioritize self-love and self-care.
- You're unwilling to compromise.
- You're reluctant to commit.
- You demand perfection from others.
- You find it difficult to accept praise or compliments.
- You aren't receptive to affection.

Opening up to love can be challenging for many reasons. We might have experienced betrayal, abuse, or neglect. We might have deep-seated fears about vulnerability and trust.

It's always scary to let people love us because to love us, they have to see us first. But receiving love helps us own our emotions. The people who love us are the very people we can trust to listen, value, and support us, no matter how we feel.

Commandment Seven: Take Responsibility for Your Emotions

EXERCISE: BOOST YOUR EMOTIONAL IQ
TIME IT TAKES: Around 30 minutes

Your emotional intelligence (EI) is how well you understand, work with, and own your feelings and emotions. Emotional intelligence exercises and activities can help boost your EI (also called your EQ–Emotional Quotient) to understand yourself and others at a deeper level.

One good way to boost your EQ is to do a temperament analysis. On the next page explore the following in writing:

1) Choose three adjectives that describe your temperament.
2) Choose three adjectives you think the people who know you best would use to describe your temperament.
3) Examine all six adjectives separately and ask: is this attribute most influenced by my environment, my life experiences, my genetic inheritance, or my physical characteristics?
4) How do each of these six attributes affect my ability to lead effectively? (This can be leading others or yourself!)
5) Do I want to transform any of these attributes? If so, why?

Once you've fully absorbed your temperament analysis, try talking it over with a friend. Get their feedback and see whether you accurately described how others see you.

Boost Your Emotional IQ

3 adjectives that describe my temperament:

3 adjectives I think others would use to describe me:

Do these 6 adjectives come from environment, life experiences, genetic inheritance, or physical qualities?

How do each of these affect my ability to lead?

Do I want to transform any of these attributes?

If so, why?

Additional Notes

Commandment Eight: Photoshop Your Self-Image

Self Image Is Not Fixed

Self-image is how you see yourself. It's the mental image–or personal view–you hold of your qualities and characteristics. While it might feel like you've held onto a fixed self-image for a long time, it's important to remember our self-image is dynamic. It can change over time.

Self-image qualities can include things like:

- Beautiful
- Ugly
- Awkward
- Selfish
- Timid
- Intelligent
- Athletic
- Funny

And on and on...

Generally, self-image is a product of learning. Parents, caregivers, peers, and teachers greatly impact how we see ourselves. These early influences are so powerful that we often hold onto outdated and faulty impressions of ourselves.

Whether we have a primarily negative or positive self-image, we must understand that we are ever-evolving. We aren't the same person we were ten or even five years ago. As such, we should regularly check in with our self-image to ensure it aligns with our reality.

No matter how you see yourself, there are several things you can do to help "photos hop" your self-image. And it's not about being fake! It's about erasing destructive perceptions and putting your best self forward.

Dress to Impress

Whether you're showing up for others–or simply showing up for yourself, dressing to impress is something you do for yourself. It means showing up in a way that makes YOU feel authentic, put together, and stylish. This habit will boost your confidence and send a message to others: You take pride in who you are, top to bottom.

Studies show that well-dressed people are more confident. They also tend to be more respected and well-received by their peers. But this doesn't mean you have to look like everyone else or conform to a specific expectation.

Dressing to impress means:

- You feel comfortable and confident.
- You can move easily and naturally.
- Your outfit choice reflects your personal taste and style.
- You accessorize in ways that make you feel beautiful.

And you don't have to spend tons of money to dress well! There are countless shops and online apps where you can purchase second-hand clothing in brand-new or like-new condition. In fact, you can often snag designer labels and high-quality pieces for at 50-70% off.

If you don't feel comfortable in heels, don't wear them. If dresses make you uncomfortable, rock your favorite pants instead. Dress how you want, in colors and styles and cuts that make you feel powerful, and you will have mastered "dressing to impress."

Confident Body Language

Video conferencing has given us an opportunity to watch ourselves, whether we wanted to or not! Turns out, seeing ourselves on camera isn't as exciting as it sounds. But it IS a great chance to observe our body language.

Whether you're on camera or not, try to pay attention to the message your body language is sending to others.

Confident body language includes:

- Eye contact.
- No fidgeting.
- Leaning in.
- Standing up straight.
- Keeping your chin up.
- Giving a firm handshake.
- Walking with authority, including larger steps.
- Keeping your hands away from your face and neck.

Now that you've identified these body language "tells," you'll be more likely to notice them in everyday life. Take deep breaths and try taking baby steps if confident body language is new territory for you.

Start by making occasional eye contact, slowing your movements, and folding fidgety hands in your lap or on the table. Over time, your internal confidence will rise to match the signals your body is sending.

The Importance of Self-Care

Taking care of your body, mind, and spirit is a powerful way to boost your self-esteem, confidence, and self-love. After all, when you abuse or neglect yourself, it does a number on your self-worth.

As you practice self-care, you'll come to appreciate that it's not just a habit; it's an at titude. And it's not one of selfishness! Unless you take care of yourself, you'll never be able to show up for others–and the world–in the way you want. The more you take care of yourself, the more happy and helpful you'll be.

Essential self-care practices include:

- Saying "no" when you've got too much on your plate.
- Orienting your life around your values.
- Creating boundaries between work and personal life.
- Asking for what you need.
- Eating healthy and getting enough exercise.
- Positive self-talk.
- Quiet time to yourself.
- Investing in yourself and your passions.

When you're kind and compassionate with yourself, you're much more likely to extend those feelings to others. It's when we're running on empty, exhausted and overwhelmed, that we start withholding and resenting those around us.

Commandment Eight: Photoshop Your Self-Image

EXERCISE: Plan Your Look In Advance
TIME IT TAKES: Around 15 minutes

Decision fatigue is real. It's what happens when there are so many options in front of you that you get tired and, usually, frustrated. One action that helps you avoid decision fatigue–and photoshop your self-image–is to lay out your wardrobe, accessories, and "look" the night before.

As with all things, being intentional about self-image makes all the difference. When you start with the basics–how you're presenting yourself to the world–it affects how you feel internally as well. It's a huge confidence and self-esteem boost with the potential to transform your entire day.

1) At the end of the day, choose your outfit for the following day. Check the weather so you can choose the right layers, shoes, and accessories. If the forecast calls for rain, locate your umbrella and rain-friendly footwear.
2) Next, pick your accessories. That includes glasses, sunglasses, socks, undergarments, hat, jewelry, scarf, etc. The more complete your look is, the more time you save in the morning.
3) Plan your skincare and makeup in advance. Depending on the day's events, are you going for a professional look, minimalist look, do you need higher SPF sunscreen, extra lip protection from cold weather, etc.

Planning tomorrow's look in detail is a great way to practice self-care for many reasons. First, you're setting yourself up for a much less stressed morning. With everything picked out, all you have to do is get ready. Second, you're sending a powerful message to yourself and others that you care about how you show up in the world.

I have provided an example on the following page to guide you in planning your daily look. Don't worry, I have also included a few empty pages for you to practice on.

Plan Your Look in Advance

TOP

BOTTOM

SHOES

ACCESSORIES

TOP

BOTTOM

SHOES

ACCESSORIES

Commandment Nine: Think Positively & Kill Negative Thoughts

What is Self-Talk?

First things first: Positive thinking is not about living in denial. It's also not about failing to take accountability or acknowledge the harsh realities of life. But think about how often your self-talk turns dark–or negative.

Does any of the following sound familiar?

- I never learn.
- I always make the same mistakes.
- No one understands me.
- I'm too old to get started.
- I'll never be good enough/smart enough/talented enough.

The question is not whether we engage in self-talk. The question is: What are we saying? More often than not, our self-talk is harsh, black-and-white, and exaggerated. But we should never accept abuse–especially from ourselves.

Left unchecked, negative thoughts shape our identity, influencing our behavior and choices. The sample thoughts above are extreme, with no room for shades of gray. If you have words like "always" and "never" running around in your brain, your self-talk needs a makeover.

Positive Counter-Arguments:

Positive thinking is more than just focusing on things that sound nice. You want to counter negative black-and-white thinking with productive and authentic state ments.

Consider the following counter-thoughts:

When you think: I never learn.
Counter with: I am learning and growing. I struggle more in some areas than others, but I continue to hold myself accountable because I value self-improvement.

When you think: I'm too old to get started.
Counter with: Not everyone's path follows the same course, and many people who made outstanding contributions were labeled late bloomers: JK Rowling, Samuel L. Jackson, Vera Wang, and Grandma Moses are just a few.

You'll notice that the positive thoughts above are much more fleshed out, reasonable, and productive. They aren't exaggerations, oversimplifications, or insults. As such, they can help you change your mind about two things: how you talk to yourself and how you feel about yourself.

Positive VS. Negative: The Impact

Positive thinking is more than just pretty words. It involves examining the tone of your current self-talk and deciding whether it's healthy, accurate, and constructive.

Replacing negative thinking with positive thinking can:

- Increase your lifespan.
- Lower levels of distress and pain.
- Support better mental health.
- Make you more resistant to illness.
- Improve psychological and physical well-being.
- Reduce the risk of death from cardiovascular disease and stroke.

As you can see, Positive thinking isn't denial–it's discernment. Your brain processes around 70,000 thoughts daily, and science shows that humans tend to replay many of the same thoughts. What ideas are you repeating?

In recent years, neuroscientists discovered that the brain can be rewired, something previously thought impossible. This ability is called neuroplasticity, which means our brain can change through growth and reorganization. Swapping corrosive thinking for inspired thinking literally rewires our brains.

Stop Negative Thoughts In Their Tracks

Changing the tone of our self-talk is hard because it's habitual. If we're used to shaming ourselves or expecting the worst, those neural pathways are well-worn in our minds. They're the roads our thoughts travel every day–our go-to responses.

Creating new paths can feel foreign and unnatural. We can't operate on auto-pilot; we must think about our thinking. But the more we travel new routes, the more established they are. Over time, we are more inclined towards positive thoughts, and our negative thinking is an overgrown path we avoid.

Many people never stop to confront the voices of shame, condemnation, and cynicism in their heads. We might think we ARE our thoughts, and we can't change them. But our thinking might come from a parent, environment, or culture, and it might not serve us.

Next time you feel inundated by negative self-talk, try to examine the narrative.

Ask yourself these questions:

- Where does this thinking come from?
- Is this my thinking or someone else's?
- How does my body feel when I sit with these thoughts?
- Am I energized or exhausted by these thoughts?
- Do these thoughts inspire me to grow?
- Would I say these things to someone I love?
- Would I say these things to a child?

If your self-talk includes statements you would never say to another person, it needs an overhaul. If sitting with your thoughts makes your body tense, inflamed, and achy, it's time to examine the contents of your self-talk.

If your self-talk was handed down to you by a parent, sibling, spouse, or someone else, it's time to take control of the narrative. When negative thoughts creep in, don't let them derail you. Speak the truth, and watch as they lose their power.

Commandment Nine: Think Positively & Kill Negative Thoughts

EXERCISE: Write a Letter to Your Younger Self
TIME IT TAKES: As long as you need

Writing a letter to your younger self is an excellent way to build self-acceptance and promote healing, both of which can help put negative thoughts in their plac[e].

First: It's natural to have mixed feelings about writing your younger self. You might feel silly or fearful of what emotions could surface. But if you see this exercise throu-gh, you'll understand why dispensing compassion and understanding to a younger you is precious.

Here are some simple guidelines:

1) Choose an age. Specificity is always essential. Pick a specific age or period so you know the YOU you're addressing. Think about where you lived, how you felt, how you looked, and where you were emotionally.

2) Reflect on your tone. Write whatever comes to mind. What advice, insight, or comfort would you give your young self? Pay attention to how you're saying these things. You'll probably be surprised by how gentle, kind, and generous your tone is. Consider how you might benefit from using this tone more often. How does it make you feel when you read your own words back in this tone?

3) Include things you wish others had taught you. This step is power-ful. You can now impart wisdom and guidance to yourself in a way others might not have. No matter your elders' parenting or teaching style, you have the authority as an adult to choose how to guide and encourage yourself.

You can write more than one letter to your younger self if you feel compelled. You probably have a lot to say! Check in with the letter regularly to see how well the tone in the letter matches your everyday internal monologue.

Generally, the gentle encouragement and guidance of the letter is the same tone we should be using as adults. We may think that hard or critical words help us improve, but they tend to have the opposite effect-whether you're seven or ninety-seven.

Turn to the next page and jot down 20 things you would share with your younger self. Believe me, both you and your younger self will appreciate it in the future.

20 Things I Would Tell My Younger Self

1	2
3	4
5	6
7	8
9	10
11	12
13	14
15	16
17	18
19	20

Commandment Ten: Don't Be Afraid to Ask for Help

Asking for Help is Hard

Some people have no trouble asking for help. But for many, the very thought of asking for help inspires discomfort. And this distress occurs on a spectrum from a minor nervous flutter to a paralyzing sense of dread.

Why Are We Afraid?

Like many beliefs, our ideas around asking for help are usually formed in childhood. Perhaps we were encouraged when we asked for help. Or, we might have been shamed. Humiliation is a potent wound–and motivator–that can impact us for life.

To make things more complicated, individualistic societies place a lot of value on self-reliance. But this emphasis can quickly become unhealthy. We might start to believe we're a burden, a failure, or weak simply because we need help.

Wherever and whenever we develop a sense of fear, pride, or shame around asking for help, these responses are emotionally damaging and only lead to self-sabotage. After all, no one can do it all on their own.

How to Get Better at Asking for Help

The good news? Asking for help is like any other skill. If you're curious and teachable, you can hone it and start seeing benefits immediately.

Asking for help could even become one of your most incredible superpowers! Let's look at three ways to get better at–and maybe even learn to love–asking for help.

Trust Science

Those who love science will be fascinated to know that plenty of research supports the benefits of asking for (and giving) help. For instance, people tend to view asking for help as a sign of competence, not weakness.

The science also shows that most people WANT to help!

Being of service can:

- Increase self-esteem.
- Boost social connection.
- Lower stress levels.
- Help us live longer.
- Promote feelings of happiness.

The idea that people might look down on us for needing help is powerful. But science also shows that it's misguided. So next time you feel like a burden, remember that most people are more than happy to lend a helping hand.

Make it a Habit

Ah, the power of a habit! What once felt foreign or out of reach becomes as familiar and natural as breathing. Well, almost!

Asking for help can become a habit, just like anything else. Ease your way into it by starting with small requests, then build your help-seeking tolerance from there. Re member, nerves are typical and might not ever go away entirely.

Ralph Waldo Emerson said, "Always do what you are afraid to do." And when it comes to asking for help, that's pretty solid advice.

Growing from "No"

Reconsidering long-help beliefs is challenging, exhilarating, and empowering. While it's scary at first, remember: You aren't your beliefs. Maybe you always thought asking for help was a sign of ignorance or laziness. Are these beliefs balanced, healthy, or productive? All questions worth exploring.

Just because you get better at asking for help doesn't mean people will always say yes. But what if you could grow from their no? "Growing from no" means reflecting on the experience, learning something, and adding that knowledge to your toolbox for future use.

For example, you might learn:

- People need more time to plan.
- The person didn't have the resources to help.
- You asked the wrong person.
- The timing was off.
- The person can't help, but they know someone who can.
- You need to tweak your request.

The Benefits of Asking for Help

Now for the fun part! Asking for help has limitless potential for benefits and advantages. If you've avoided asking for help your whole life, making it a habit could transform your future in ways you never imagined.

Here are just a few benefits of asking for help:

- Build important connections.
- Grow and evolve as a person.
- Protect yourself from burnout and overwhelm.
- Build rejection resilience.
- Increase productivity.
- Achieve much more than ever before.
- Contribute to a positive culture.

The benefits of asking for help can't be overstated because everyone who ever did anything significant needed help–probably lots of it.

The most impactful social movements, businesses, and even works of art all have one thing in common: They reached incredible heights with a lot of help from a lot of people. That means somewhere along the way, someone had to...

You guessed it: **ASK!**

Commandment Ten: Don't Be Afraid to Ask for Help

EXERCISE: Log Your Asks
Time it takes: A few minutes

Tracking why and how you've asked for help alongside the short-term and long-term results can help you collect valuable data on the effects of your "asks."

Whether you asked for additional training, emotional support, a financial investment, or more time on a task, try to track your journey of becoming more and more comfortable asking for help.

As you do, you'll be able to see the benefits, rewards, and impact in each instance. Hopefully, it will feel like charting a map forward - one that includes fearlessness around asking other people to lend a helping hand.

Log these items:

1) The Ask
2) How did I feel before and after asking?
3) What was the immediate response/result?
4) Did the person respond as I expected?
5) Regardless of their answer, did I learn anything from the experience?
6) If they said no, is there someone else I can ask? And/or, would it be better to ask later?

Don't forget to return to each "ask" a few weeks later to update: are there any new developments regarding this ask? If so, note them. By writing them down, you'll start to see patterns in your own behavior as well as how others are responding to you, which is an education of its own!

Start your log on the next page. Keep in mind that there's no need to hesitate when asking for what you want. Remember, as the saying goes, those who don't speak up often miss out on opportunities.

Log Your Asks

What is the ask?

How did I feel before asking? And after?

What was the immediate response/result?

Was the response what I expected?

Did I learn anything from the experience?

If the answer was no, is there someone else I can ask?

Additional Notes

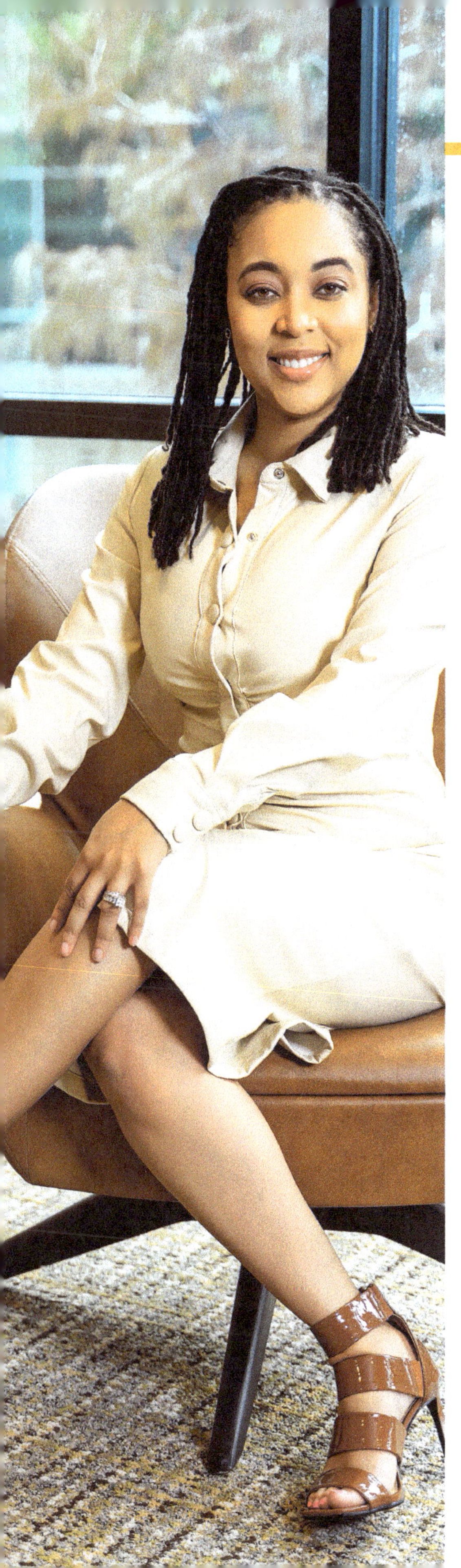

Meet the Author

Dr. J. Caldwell is a confidence architect and business strategist whose work focus on identity, emotional intelligence and personal alignment as the foundation for sustainable growth.

A Houston native, Dr. J. Caldwell brings years over 15 of experience across corporate leadership, human resources, and organizational development. Her professional journey, spanning high-growth industries and complex people systems, deepened her understanding of a simple truth: confidence is not a personality trait, title, or outcome. It is an internal operating system.

The 10 Confidence Commandments was born not as a business manual or leadership framework, but as a personal journal, written during seasons of transition, self-reflection, and recalibration. These principles were lived long before they were shared, shaped by real experiences navigating boundaries, purpose, emotional responsibility, and self-trust.

Dr. J. Caldwell is the founder of She NetWORTH, an empowerment platform created to help individuals, particularly women and underrepresented communities, reclaim confidence, clarity, and self-worth in both life and work. While her professional work continues to evolve, her commitment remains the same: helping people strengthen the internal foundation that makes sustainable success possible.

Through her writing and speaking, Dr. J. Caldwell explores how confidence, identity, and emotional intelligence shape long-term personal fulfillment and meaningful impact.

The Confidently M.A.D.E. Journey

Being Confidently M.A.D.E. (Marvelous All Day Everyday) is not a destination, it is a commitment you return to repeatedly.

These commandments are not meant to be mastered once and set aside. They are meant to be revisited during new seasons, difficult transitions, and moments when clarity feels just out of reach.

Confidence is built through awareness.
Through responsibility.
Through aligned choices made quietly, consistently, and honestly.
At the end of each month, or whenever life invites reflection, pause and consider how each commandment is showing up for you. Notice what feels strong. Acknowledge what feels tender. Growth does not require perfection; it requires presence.
The work is internal.
The responsibility is personal.
The journey is ongoing.
Confidence is not something you wait to feel.
It is something you practice; one aligned choice at a time.

– Dr. J. Caldwell

www. drjcaldwell. com

www.ingramcontent.com/pod-product-compliance
Lightning Source LLC
LaVergne TN
LVHW080206180826
845678LV00023BA/1756

* 9 7 9 8 8 6 8 9 3 5 6 4 0 *